YOUR WONDERFUL FACE

A Great Start to Being Confident and Inclusive

by Conrad Wallace
Illustrated by Jupiters Muse

Your Wonderful Face
Copyright © 2022 by Conrad Wallace

Tellwell Talent
www.tellwell.ca

ISBN
978-0-2288-7291-7 (Hardcover)
978-0-2288-7290-0 (Paperback)

SECTION 1

Your Wonderful Hair

Hair is black; hair is gray.
Red or blonde—they're all fair play!
Hair is curly; hair is straight.
Each head of hair has distinct traits.

Some hair sticks up, while some lay low.
It all depends on how yours grow.
Some strands are bouncy; some are flat.
But every hair can wear a hat!

Hair gives us warmth, along with beanies.
You can style it like the genies!
Grab a comb or sturdy brush,
Or do a fro when in a rush.

We wash our hair to keep it clean
And take the knots from in between.
We add styles to give it flair.
"I love my hair!" I must declare.

Hair, hair, an awesome thing.
What new fashion will yours bring?
Wear it high or wear it low.
Wear it proud wherever you go!

SECTION 2

Your Wonderful Eyes

Eyes can be big, medium, or tiny.
They see in front and not behind me.
Eyes are brown, and some are blue.
Eyes are green, and grey eyes too.

Eyes are for seeing, not to taste.
Eyes are found atop my face.
Eyes see near and they see far.
I use my eyes to see a star.

Eyes are wide, eyes are narrow.
I squint to see a baby sparrow.
Eyes are drooped when they get tired.
They let you know sleep is required.

Food for eyes: carrots and kale,
to keep them well and never fail.
Eyes drip tears when they cry,
but sometimes feel a little dry.

Eyes see hands that wave goodbye.
Eyes see balloons float in the sky.
For all the stunning things you see,
eyes are great you must agree!

SECTION 3

Your Wonderful Ears

They're big on elephants, small on moles.
Close to my eyes, not to my toes.
These are my ears; use them to hear.
I don't have one; I have a pair.

They hear loud bangs; they hear a squeak.
They hear the door hinge when they creak.
They listen to oceans from seashells.
If there are sounds, my ears can tell.

By using all its many sections,
ears can listen to directions.
Outer, middle, inner ear too.
They work together, it is true.

The wax they trap, so dust can't pass.
The way ears work is unsurpassed.
They cannot see, that's for my eyes.
But to listen, ears will win first prize!

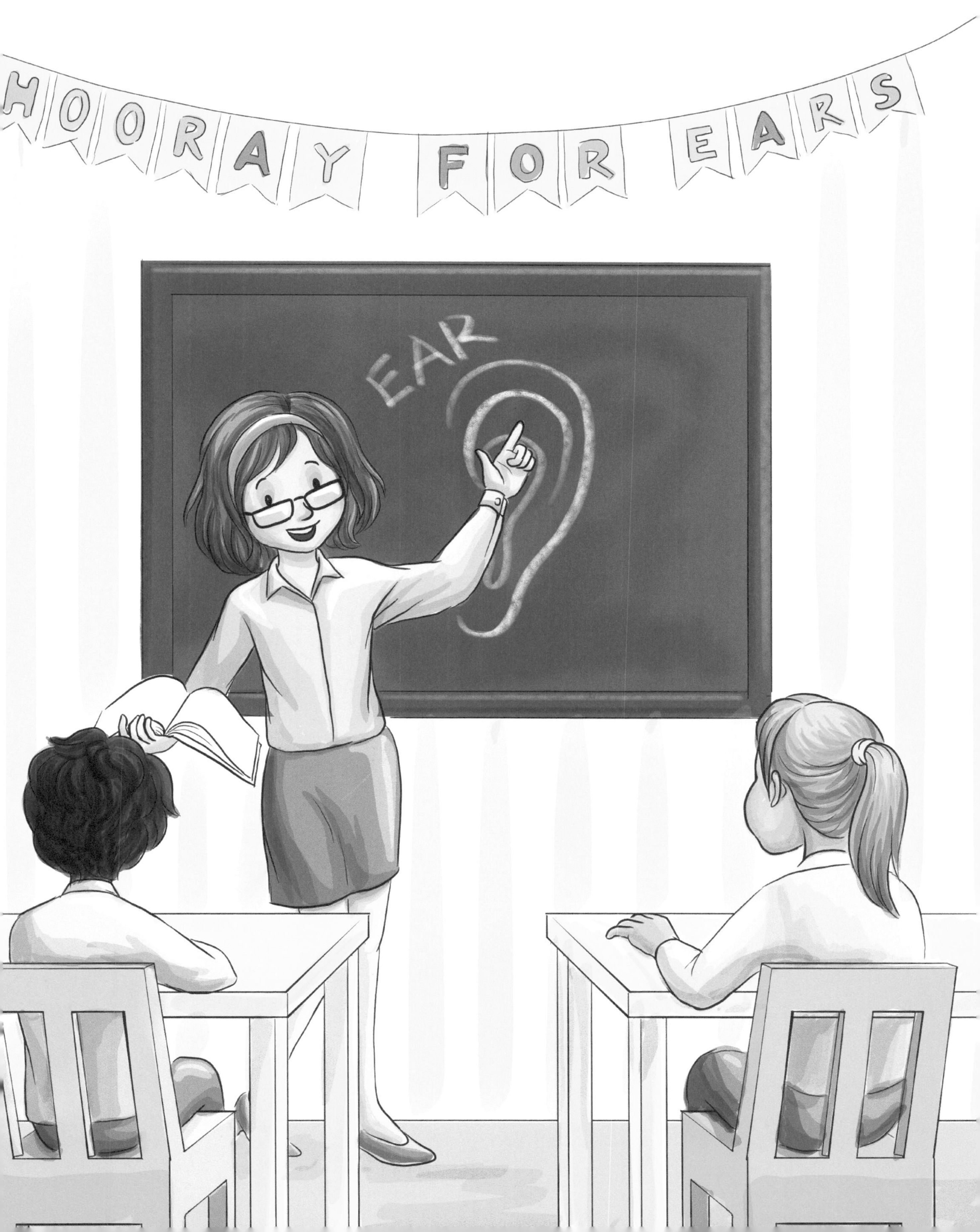
HOORAY FOR EARS
EAR

Ears are wonderful, big, or small.
I'm thankful for my ears that's all.
I'll care for them; keep volumes down.
My ears are the best, I have found!

SECTION 4

Your Wonderful Nose

What is that scent, can you tell?
What do you use to sniff and smell?
It is your nose! Awesome guess!
For smelling things, it is the best!

Noses are straight, crooked, or clunky.
Sometimes they are a little chunky.
They can be sniffly, stuffy, or runny.
Noses can twitch just like a bunny!

Noses are useful to inhale
and breathe fresh air on mountain trails.
Noses have hairs that cling and trap,
the dirt and grime that passed that gap.

Noses have mucus! Not all bad.
It protects our lungs; I'd like to add.
Noses are greater than you think.
Through our nose, we breathe, while we drink.

Despite the shape or style of your nose,
It is great and everyone knows.
So, wear it proud; wear it strong.
It's the one you'll carry your whole life long.

SECTION 5

Your Wonderful Mouth

My favored thing is to sing and shout,
From the thing below my nose - my mouth!
Your mouth can sing, shout, and talk.
They even work when we walk!

Mouths will laugh and mouths will cry.
Sometimes they'll give a lengthy sigh.
Mouths are clean, but they get messy,
especially when they eat spaghetti!

Mouths are best friends with round spoons.
They're also great for whistling tunes.
Babies' mouths like binkies – that's so cute!
They also love their yummy fruits.

Mouths have teeth; they have a tongue.
Clean and white and pink and long.
Mouths will drink and they will feed.
Sometimes they move when you read.

Love your mouth and care it too.
Use it to speak what is true.
Your mouth is great, use it for good
And say kind things as we all should.

Lightning Source UK Ltd.
Milton Keynes UK
UKHW050937170223
417094UK00002B/82